HOME SECURITY: THE SECURE DAD'S GUIDE

Easy Home Defense Techniques to Keep Your Family Safe

Andy Murphy

Cover by: Amy Brandt
www.amybrandtdesigns.com

The Secure Dad, LLC
www.thesecuredad.com

ISBN-13:
978-1719571913
ISBN-10:
1719571910

Contents

Free Bonus

Thank you for your interest in this book and The Secure Dad. To make the most of your reading experience, I've created a printable home security checklist to help you apply the techniques in the book and make small, intentional steps to help you in making your home and family safer. Simply go to www.thesecuredad.com/checklist-for-readers today.

For my family. Thank you for all your unwavering support.

INTRODUCTION: WHAT IS THE SECURE DAD?

I know how you feel. You love your family. They are the most valuable thing in your life, and you want to protect them the best way possible. But there's a fine line between being safe and being scared. I am the same way. That's why I started The Secure Dad.

Life Changing Event

Growing up, I'd been taught, like you, to Stop, Drop and Roll if I caught on fire. I'd been told to stay in school and say no to drugs. And I was told that if I were in trouble to call 911. That's it.

Now what I was supposed to do until the police showed up, I had no idea. I had been conditioned to think that when my life was in danger I needed to call the police and they'd magically be there to save me. This is an impossible standard in which to hold our brave first responders. Ask any police officer, and they'll tell you they can't be everywhere all the time. It's just not humanly possible.

One afternoon in April 1999, I came home and turned on the news. My screen was filled with images of high schoolers marching out of their school with their hands over their heads. As I sat and listened, I learned of the horror that had taken place at Columbine High School. While I wasn't there, my life changed forever.

All those kids on the news looked like my friends and me. I could easily see myself in them. It was an uncomfortable feeling. I had never thought

1

that students could plan and execute a school attack. My mind just didn't work that way.

This was when my mindset began to change. I realized that if someone in my classroom started attacking us, there would be no realistic way our school resource officer could get to us in time. Some of us, maybe me, would be hurt or dead by the time he arrived.

This was when I realized that my safety is my own responsibility. From that moment I began to develop a secure mindset that would make me and those I love safer.

The Uncomfortable Truth

Every family wants to be safe. But not every family proactively takes ownership of their own safety. That's a big problem facing many families. It's perfectly normal to want to feel safe. When we go to sleep at night, we want to rest assured that our home is going to keep us safe from the elements and intruders. But to sleep well at night, we must know our home and that our family is prepared to act if necessary. This requires a change in thinking. We now have to face the uncomfortable truth that someone might hurt our family. That's a scary thought, I know.

Many families don't want to think about their safety because to do so they must accept that something bad could happen to them. I call this living in a bubble. Inside this bubble, everyone has a well-paying job, everyone lives by the Golden Rule, and a police officer will appear out of thin air when they need one. I wish this were true, but the real world doesn't work that way.

I think all of us as parents need to realize that just by thinking about how to save your family from a house fire doesn't mean that we're going to set it ablaze. It's not morbid to think about what to do when you smell smoke. It's careless not to think about a fire escape plan until you're on fire. We can't protect our families effectively if we are not prepared.

Being prepared doesn't mean we make our home a prison with bars on the windows. It doesn't mean we ignore our neighbors, living behind closed blinds. It doesn't call for us to live in fear. Having a secure mindset means we courageously live our lives with confidence. Confidence in knowing that we can manage a threat to our home and keep our loved ones safe.

Having a secure mindset is a balance between knowing how to defend your home while playing football in the front yard.

The Secure Dad

I started The Secure Dad because I have a genuine desire to give families the information they can use to become safer. I'm not an expert in the field of security or situational awareness nor am I a member of the law enforcement community or military. But as I have demonstrated with more than 100 articles on TheSecureDad.com, I am a man who woke up to the basic human fact that my safety and my family's safety is my responsibility.

Some may question how I can tell anyone about security because I'm just a dad. But that is the problem the plagues our society. Police officer, and author, Robert J. Disario says it this way in his book *Protect Yourself*, "We have become dependent on technology and government to protect us, almost relinquishing control to others. We need to take ownership of our own safety." Disario is right, and that's just what I've done.

I've made personal and family safety the study of my life. I've read many fascinating books, listened to my intuition, talked with law enforcement personnel, taken multiple self-defense classes, attended security seminars and practiced what I have preached since 1999.

There is no "one size fits all" answer to family protection and home security. It would be impossible for me to predict all the specific events that may threaten your family. I can't even predict the potential threats I may face, that's just a fact of life. But to counter this uncertainty, we must be prepared to act in whatever way necessary to keep us safe.

You need to know that if someone wants to break into your home bad enough, they will find a way inside. That's a scary thought. Understand that I'm not going to suggest that you make your home impenetrable. In fact, you'll later read why I don't recommend that at all. The purpose of this book is to help you stage your home to deter a break-in in the first place and buy time to protect your family if an invasion occurs while you are home.

In the following chapters, we will go over how to act with your new mindset, fortify your home, and how to minimize the chances of your home being targeted for a crime in the first place. Take the ideas shared in this book and customize them to your lifestyle, your home, and your family. The purpose of this book is to provide you with the information you need to make more informed decisions about your family's safety.

I believe that a secure life resides in serving a loving God who will guide you and your family daily. Knowing my life is in the hands of a merciful God who loves me, gives me strength and security every day. The book is a direct result of God's calling for my life. "It is God who arms me with strength and keeps my way secure." (Psalm 18:32 NIV)

The Secure Dad empowers fathers to lead safer, more secure families giving them the freedom to enjoy the blessings of life. I want you to understand how you can make your family safer in small steps. To be able to evaluate potential threats and respond accordingly. To live life free from worry because you are prepared.

How to Become Immediately Safer

Most Americans drift from place to place in life without a thought of their personal safety, let alone the security of their family. I see it every day. People with their faces glued to their phones not caring about who is only 18 inches away from them and ignoring what that person might do to them. Chances are if you are reading this book, you've been this person before and love someone that is this way now.

Secure Dad Action Tip: Start to notice how close you let people get to you. Then watch others who aren't paying attention to their surroundings. See if you can sense how easy a target people can be when they aren't concerned about protecting themselves.

Why do some people freely give away their personal safety to others? Maybe they don't think crime can happen to them? They believe their house is safe because it's in a "nice" area of town. They post their vacation photos while they're out of the country, not once thinking about the information they're giving away.

All of these are real rationales. What normal, well-adjusted people need to understand is that they lack the thought process to be an attacker. That's good. But that is precisely why they don't see the need to keep themselves safe. They can't imagine why someone would want to harm them, so they assume by default they are safe. This is false security based on ignorance.

Look at the local paper or a news station website. The people whose homes were ransacked today didn't think anything bad was going to happen to them. But there they are. No one thinks it's going to happen to them or their family, but the fact is that good people are hurt every day.

When I explain the steps I take to be safe some people may think I'm overreacting to...nothing. That's not true. There's nothing wrong with realizing you can be a target for crime. It's human nature to want to stay safe and alive.

Those who seek to protect themselves and their homes are simply doing what our instinct or intuition tells us to do. For thousands of years, humanity has been living to stay alive and safe. Just because you hunt and gather at Starbucks doesn't mean this core fact of life has changed.

People may assume since crime is trending downwards that they are safe. Don't gamble with your family's life based on last year's numbers from other states. That data on victims of violent crime comes from real people. Realize right now that statistics don't mean anything when a burglar has kicked in your door. Your personal commitment to protecting yourself is your best option.

The good news is that there is one thing that you can do today to live a safer life: change your mindset.

With a secure mindset, you'll know to look for strangers in your neighborhood. You will understand the importance of putting your lights on timers when you go on vacation. When someone knocks on your door, you'll instinctively know to look out of the door viewer to see who is there.

Using this newfound knowledge to your advantage can influence daily decisions for the better. When your mindset is changed to put safety first, you can be ready to instinctively make safer decisions thus making your home safer.

Beginning to think about your safety and practicing simple protection techniques means you're less likely to be a victim. From now on you'll know to shift focus to your safety when you're home enjoying life. The key to decreasing crime in the United States isn't law enforcement response time or more security cameras. The key to making America safer is to realize we have a culture with violent influences and can respond to it accordingly by changing the way we see ourselves in our world.

In his book, *Protecting the Gift: Keeping Children and Teenagers Safe (and Parents Sane)* author Gavin de Becker writes; "Because the solution to violence in America is not more laws, more guns, more police, or more prisons. The solution to violence is acceptance of reality." We need to understand that we are a violent nation. We can't keep denying this fact. Once we accept it, we can embrace a change in mindset to keep our families safe.

There isn't a "one size fits all" product that is a solution to home or family security. That includes this book. You can read it, but it won't do you any good until you put into practice what is discussed here. Once you understand these fundamental principles of family and home security, everything else begins to make sense.

You might ask if a change in mindset will make you paranoid. The short answer that it shouldn't. Remember what you learned first about fire safety? If you caught on fire, you learned to stop, drop and roll. Your brain filed that information away, confident in your ability to put yourself out if you had to. But you didn't become paranoid about fire, right? You didn't let stop, drop and roll consume your life and steal your joy. Having a secure mindset works the same way.

I've been using a secure mindset for half my life. I'm not a scared father. I'm not in fear for my family's safety. I am confident in my abilities as a protector. This mindset gives me the courage, the freedom, to enjoy the blessings of my life.

This book isn't going to guarantee your family's safety. No one can guarantee your safety. You can't guarantee it, and neither can law enforcement. But what this book can do is be a resource for you to live a safer, more enjoyable life by preparing your home for a potential invasion.

I'll walk you through how to make sure your home is safer, what you can do to keep from becoming a target, and how to make your family safer in the event of a home invasion. The following chapters can help you develop your own unique secure mindset.

Secure Dad Action Tip: Any time you leave your house, look around. Notice the cars that belong to your neighbors. Is there a random car parked on the street? Do all the cars belong here? Simple details like this will grow into valuable skills for a secure mindset.

CHAPTER 1: HOME SECURITY BASICS: WHAT YOU CAN DO TODAY

As I mentioned before, there is no "one size fits all" product to keep your life and home secure. It really does depend on your mindset. If you don't have a secure mindset, then leaving your car doors unlocked and your windows open isn't going to wave a red flag for you.

When you change your perspective, you'll understand that you need to close your windows and keep the doors locked. But simple everyday things begin to stand out as being unsafe, and you can instinctively change those habits.

According to the FBI, 71% of all burglaries in the United States in 2015 were in homes. Of those, 57.9% of involved forcible entry. Here are some good security habits to put into practice today to keep you from becoming part of those statistics.

Available Resources

The first simple rule of home security is to use the existing defenses your home currently has. At the top of the list are your door locks. Yes, that may seem simpler than basic, but we're starting at the beginning.

Whether living in an apartment or a house, use the existing locks. This means locking all doors when not in use. Most crimes on residences occur through the front and back door. Many of those doors are unlocked. Develop a routine of locking exterior doors every time you enter and exit your home. Don't make it easy for thieves.

Deadbolt Locks

Make sure all exterior doors have working deadbolt locks installed. A simple knob lock isn't going to provide much protection from a determined intruder. If you have deadbolt locks installed, great, let's make sure they are functioning properly.

Open the door and turn the bolt to the locked position with the deadbolt protruding from the door. Pay attention to two things: first does the deadbolt feel as if it has locked in place at its furthest point out? Can it be moved by pushing on it or is it locked in place? Second, listen for a click of the deadbolt locking in place. Reset the lock and close the door.

With the door now closed, turn the lock and pay attention to how far the deadbolt extends inside the doorframe. Be sure to listen for the clicking sound of it locking into place. If you hear and feel that it is locked, then you're good to go. Sometimes the hole in the doorframe isn't deep enough for the deadbolt to fully extend.

If this is the case, the hole needs to be deepened for the deadbolt to function properly. If the deadbolts on the door are not locking properly, then they are not providing adequate safety.

Secure Dad Action Tip: Go right now and check all of the deadbolts in your home to make sure they are functioning correctly. If not, call a professional to fix any issues.

Sliding Glass Door

I'm not a fan of sliding glass doors. They are a pain to clean and hard to secure. I had one in an apartment once. It caused me a lot of anxiety to think that someone could walk up to the glass, peek through the shades and break in quickly. But, if you've got one and have to keep it, you need a plan.

The first thing to do when securing a sliding glass door is to lock it. Yes, again I know this is basic, but we start with baby steps. Next, brace the sliding portion of the door by placing a wooden dowel in the track of the door. Get a big, thick dowel that is at least an inch wide and cut it to fit the sliding track. When you are using the door, make sure you store the dowel outside of the track, don't just lean it up against the side. The dowel can slip back down onto the track and lock you out! Ask me how I know.

Lastly, you can install a window sensor. This sensor can be a part of your alarm system or an inexpensive standalone that emits an ear-splitting siren. Either way, the movements of the burglar should be made known to anyone inside your home.

Windows

You may think that since no one can tell if a window is locked from the street, then no one will try to open it. That's wrong. Windows are the second most entered ways into residences for burglaries.

First-floor windows are to be locked at all times unless they are open, and you are home to monitor them. This includes basement windows as well. Second-floor windows should only be opened if someone is home. Don't ever leave home with an open window. A resourceful thief can steal a ladder from a neighbor's open garage and use it to access your open window. From there they can ransack your home and walk right out the front door with your valuables.

Here's another way someone can enter your home through a window that you most likely never thought about. If you have a window AC unit in your home, this can be an open invitation for a burglar. Many window AC units can be pushed from the outside and forced out of the window, falling inside. This makes a nice-sized hole for someone to enter your home. I've personally seen this happen, but not to worry, these units can be made more secure.

An inexpensive security upgrade would be a dowel rod that is added to the top of the open portion of the window. Just like a brace for a sliding glass door. The dowel should keep the window from opening further allowing the unit to be shoved from the outside. Lastly, you can install a window alarm that detects movement or vibration. These alarms are usually standalone products that trigger a siren when tripped.

Secure Dad Action Tip: Check to make sure all of your windows are currently locked. Then plan to check them regularly to avoid a potential problem.

Existing Lighting

Your home may already have a powerful theft deterrent installed on it right now, a porch light. Darkness is a thief's best ally in an assault on your home. Take away that ally by adding light to entryways.

Start tonight by deterring a front door kick-in style attack by simply turning on the porch light and leaving it on all night. After checking your doors before going to bed, turn on the porch light, too. If you're worried about forgetting to turn it on or leaving it on all day, there is an easy, inexpensive solution.

The best solution for this lighting situation is a dusk-to-dawn light bulb. These specialty bulbs are readily available on Amazon. These bulbs have a sensor embedded in it that can tell when the sun has set and when it rises. Then it turns the bulb on and off accordingly. Installation is as simple as screwing in a light bulb and flipping the switch.

Operating it is as easy as turning the switch to the on position and walking away. As long as the fixture supplies power to the dusk-to-dawn bulb, everything should work fine. This a great way to upgrade the security for an apartment or property that you can't make upgrades to without a landlord's permission.

Also, if you're concerned that you may turn the switch off by accident, install a switch guard to prevent it from being turned off. Switch guards use the existing screws in the switch plate and cover a single switch to keep it in the desired position.

Secure Dad Action Tip: Tonight, go and stand in your yard and see how dark your home appears. Then map out places you can add additional lighting to make your home look brighter to repel thieves.

Your Yard

The bushes and other plants on your property can be a great hiding place for a thief. If shrubbery is kept tall, then a full-grown man can have a great place to hide. From a hidden, close proximity, a thief can check to see if windows and doors are unlocked. They can also wait for you to arrive home and attack as you walk to the front door. Once they have control of you, they can use your keys to enter your home and use you as a hostage to keep everyone inside under their control.

By keeping the shrubs trimmed, you eliminate a hiding place. And if you have a green thumb, consider planting rose bushes under windows and by doors. Thorny plants can deter anyone from hiding in them.

Another way your yard can prevent crime is by keeping it maintained. An unkempt yard may give the impression that the home may be unoccupied. Also, it could be assumed that if the homeowner isn't diligent enough to cut the grass a few times a month, then they probably don't worry about locking their windows or back door. Regardless of the conclusion, an overgrown yard would supply hiding places for thieves and unwanted attention. Sorry guys, you have to cut the grass.

Alarm Company Signs

While on the subject of lawn decor, many people, police included, suggest putting an alarm company sign in your yard. This can be done regardless of whether an alarm system is installed or not. Generic signs can be purchased online or in home improvement stores.

The thinking here is that a person who may be on the edge of committing a crime would be deterred by the sign. A simple yard sign may not be enough to stop a determined thief. I suggest you be smart in this situation.

For example, if you have an alarm system from a big-name company, do not put their sign in the yard. Instead, purchase a generic surveillance sign and post it. Of course, these home security companies want their sign in your yard for free advertising. However, there's a downside.

When a determined thief scouts a home, he can use an online search to check an alarm system for flaws and known issues. How does this thief know the name of the company? The homeowner posted a big sign in the yard giving him all the information he needed to plan his attack. Don't give away vital information like this to potential thieves.

There is a less tech-savvy way to bypass an alarm system. When a determined thief targets a home, he will try and learn as much as he needs to get in and out easily. If a targeted home has an alarm company sign in the yard, then he's a leg up on the homeowner already.

A quick internet search can determine the home's phone number and the name of the owner. From here our thief calls the homeowner in the middle of the night posing as a representative of the company. The call may go something like this:

Thief: This is Terry at Generic Home Security, we've got a distress call from your residence. Are you okay?

Homeowner [Dazed from waking up]: Um... The alarm is not going off here.

Thief: Who am I speaking with?

Homeowner: I'm Anthony Smith, the homeowner.

Thief: Right, we got a distress call from your interface system Mr. Smith. Did someone signal a distress call?

Mr. Smith: Uh no.

Thief: Well Mr. Smith if you are okay then we need to turn this alarm off. I can easily take care of this for you. If you can just tell me your code word, I'll turn it off from my station.

Mr. Smith: Okay, great: the code word is bacon.

Thief: Ok, thank you, Mr. Smith. That seems to have settled everything down. Thanks for taking my call. Sorry for the false alarm.

Mr. Smith: Yes, thank you.

Now Mr. Smith has given away his security code word so that the scammers can break into his home and give the real code word to the real alarm company. The alarm company won't call the police if the real code word and homeowner's name is given. Don't give away this kind of information.

Controlled Access

Many families have multiple people coming and going from their home. Some people make the mistake of using a key hider to provide access when they are not home. While a little gnome leaning on a mushroom is cute for the yard, key hiders are a terrible idea. Yes, even the ones that look like rocks can be spotted quickly.

Key hiders can be spotted from the street, increasing your home's likelihood of being targeted for a crime. Also, they don't protect your key at all. They are made of cheap plastic and can be smashed open easily. And this same advice goes for leaving a key under a doormat or hidden anywhere else in your yard. There is a much safer solution to control access to your home, a keypad door lock.

These locks have ten-button keypads for codes to unlock a single door. Multiple codes can be assigned to people and codes can be permanent or temporary allowing greater flexibility for controlling access to your home. These locks are easy to install and look great on any door.

They are usually powered by a nine-volt battery and provide a manual key override. The buttons on the lock should change color to let you know the battery needs to be replaced well before it stops functioning. These locks are a great way to secure your door and allow access when and where you want.

Basic steps can make your home safer; you don't have to make your home a fortress. So, cancel that ditch digger to build that moat this weekend. Your home is the place for your family to live comfortably and safely.

CHAPTER 2: A LAYERED HOME DEFENSE STRATEGY

I remember playing with action figures as a kid. I would create elaborate battle scenes for the rebels and the empire. Part of my strategy was a layered defense using starships, physical barriers, and snipers. I did this because I wanted the rebels to do everything they could to keep the empire out and prevent fighting at close quarters. Maybe I've always been this way.

When I started thinking about my home defense as an adult, those concepts came in handy. As a protector, I want to do everything I can to prevent having a physical encounter with an intruder at close proximity inside my home.

Being prepared is key to your safety and the safety of your family. A fully developed plan is what helps families stay alive in potentially deadly situations. When the house is on fire is not the time to draw up a fire escape plan. When smoke is choking the air and lives are on the line is when you need to act, not strategize.

Imagine your family is asleep when you hear a bump in the night. The bump turns into a crash and the alarm ISN'T going off. Your mind is racing, and your heart is pounding. How did this happen? You put the alarm company sign in the yard! Isn't that supposed to stop break-ins? Did I forget to set the alarm? Where are my kids? Where is the intruder?

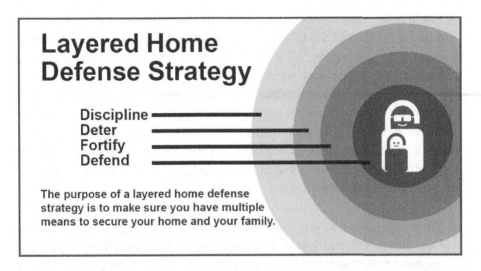

The purpose of a layered home defense strategy is to make sure you have multiple means to secure your home and your family. There are four layers to this strategy: Discipline, Deter, Fortify and Defend.

Discipline refers to what you do every day to make sure your home isn't a target for a crime. Deter are the steps you can take to communicate to a potential bad guy that this will be a tough home to burglarize and it's best if he moves on. Fortify is beefing up your physical security so that if deterring doesn't work, breaking-in will be extremely difficult. The last step in the process is defend. This is when you'll have to physically defend your family from an attacker.

It's important to know that if an intruder wants to get into your home, they can find a way in. The point of a layered home defense strategy is to deter a break-in from happening but also to help you buy time for your family in the event of a home invasion. During this precious time, your family can shelter in a safe place, police can respond, and if enough obstacles are placed in the intruder's way, he can use this time to flee.

The Adversarial Mindset

Simply put, the adversarial mindset is thinking like a bad guy. While this mindset is not part of the layered home defense strategy, it is imperative to embrace it so that you can fully develop your plan. You need this mindset to help make your home more secure.

When it comes to home security, you need to use the adversarial mindset to figure out how YOU would break into YOUR home. That's right, put yourself in a burglar's shoes. What are your home's biggest weaknesses or exploits? Where could someone hide in your yard? What time of day would you try to force your way inside?

When you, as a bad guy, have simulated breaking into your home, you will see things differently. How long will it take from your entry point to get to the master bedroom? This can provide you with a more realistic time a bad guy should have to find you in your home. Use this time to help develop your defense plan which will be discussed later.

Once you focus on this and ask yourself some uncomfortable questions, then you can start to truly secure your home. You'll discover a wealth of information just by shifting your thought process. As we discuss the layered home defense strategy, keep thinking like a bad guy.

Secure Dad Action Tip: Think about your adversarial mindset. How would you break into your home?

Are you ready for the bump in the night? The best way to approach protecting your house is by instituting a layered home defense strategy: Discipline, Deter, Fortify and Defend.

CHAPTER 3: LAYERED HOME DEFENSE STRATEGY: DISCIPLINE

The outermost layer of the layered home defense strategy starts with personal discipline for basic behaviors. The actual point of the discipline layer of this strategy is to prevent the chance of creating the opportunity for a crime to be committed against you.

Every day we need to commit to simple behaviors that will keep our family safe. This means taking ownership of how your actions affect your safety daily. This can keep your home from being targeted for a crime in the first place.

Believe it or not, there are simple things that we do that can tell a bad guy your home will be an easy target. When you leave the garage door open with no cars inside, you're telling someone there's no one home. Small things like this can add up to make your home an easy target for a thief.

Social Media

According to Nationwide Insurance, four out of five burglars say they use social media to target homes. Let that sink in. People are arming burglars with the information they need to target their own homes. You need to begin to think critically about what you put on social media and how it will affect your home and family security.

You may not realize it, but frequently we broadcast valuable information about our family and schedules to the public. If you've ever checked in at a coffee shop, then you've told everyone where you are. But the information you are giving away is that you are currently not at home.

Vacation Pictures

If you're going on a great trip, save the pictures until you get back. Do not go live on social media while standing on the deck of a cruise ship. Everyone can figure out that you are not at home. Don't make things easy for a burglar.

Leaving your home for an extended amount of time is a secret most people understand. But the connection isn't made when a person posts that they are loving their balcony view of the Atlantic Ocean and therefore has told everyone that their house in Kansas is vacant.

If you must share pictures of your trip while you're on it, then I have an idea for you. When my family went to Disney, we didn't post pictures on social media until we got back. But we did text pictures to our parents, so they could see the fun we were having.

This way we felt good about sharing photos but also knew our travel plans would remain secret. Consider picking a trusted family member or friend to share pictures with while you are on your trip. Then post them to social media once you are back home.

Secure Dad Action Tip: Call yourself out here. If you've taken photos on a trip and posted them in real time, you need to stop. I know vacations are fun, but no one wants to return to a ransacked home.

What we need to understand about posting our plans on social media is this: we are actively giving away valuable information. Bad guys aren't stealing it; we are openly offering it for free on a public forum. We need to use the adversarial mindset as a part of our discipline when posting online.

Ask yourself two things before your next post: 1) What am I saying in this post? 2) What am I unintentionally saying in this post?

For example, you decide to vent a little about your kid's soccer practice schedule:

"The new soccer season has started for Madison. That means weekly practices again. Ugh. Guess where I'll be every Thursday night until June?"

When we analyze this post, we get that you're not happy with giving up your time to sit and watch your kid practice soccer. But we also know that soccer practice is held on Thursday nights until June. That means you'll be at the soccer field and no one will be at home next Thursday night. You just gave a burglar a timeframe to strike your home.

Try to avoid posting pictures of your newest possessions on social media. It may be hard to resist posting a picture of your beautiful new riding lawnmower, but you don't want to draw negative attention to your possessions. Couple this with the post that reveals when you're not home and you've set up when, where, and what could be stolen from you.

As another example, you choose to show off a picture of your new riding lawnmower before you leave for vacation:

"Check out this beauty! It's got a sweet zero-turn radius. Can't wait to cut the grass next week when we come back from the beach."

When we look at this post, we understand that you're proud of your new lawn mower. But we also know that it's going to be unattended while you're at the beach. So now a thief knows to bring a trailer with him when he robs your home.

Secure Dad Action Tip: Analyze your past posts on social media. See where you've checked in, what events you've said you were interested in, and what pictures you've shared while on location. Start changing the way you post online.

Business Trips

If you're on a business trip away from your wife and kids, don't let anyone know that you are unavailable to protect them. While the lights in your home are on as usual and cars are going in and out, you still don't need to let anyone know you're gone. This is not a slight against mothers or their ability to defend their homes or children. The term "Mama Bear" exists for a reason.

Potential intruders can capitalize on one adult being home. It can be much easier for them to control the house if they know there is only one person who can fight back. Don't give the bad guys any information they can use to make a plan to attack your home.

Crime You Create

The discipline layer of our home defense strategy also motivates us to eliminate opportunities for our homes to be targeted for a crime. Opportunity-based crime is when a person commits an illegal act without planning, the environmental conditions are favorable for a crime to occur and the perpetrator perceives a low risk of being caught. No premeditation is involved; the bad guy saw a chance to commit a crime with little risk of being caught in the act.

So, what is a good example of a crime of opportunity? The most obvious one is stealing a car that is parked in your driveway with the windows down and the keys in the ignition. All that is required is simply getting into the car and driving off.

It's not a hard crime to commit, and the likelihood of getting caught in the act is very low. Simply stated, the perpetrator saw an opportunity to make a significant gain (the car) with little resistance to the act (the windows being down in an empty car and keys inside).

In this scenario, who is to blame? The perpetrator, for sure, as no criminal act HAD to take place. No one has to steal a car. Leaving the car parked with the windows down and the keys inside is irresistible to a certain criminal element.

Is the car owner to blame as well? Legally, the answer is no. That said, the owner created an opportunity for their property to be stolen easily. The only person responsible for keeping your property secure is you.

I know a couple who live in a nice neighborhood. There was a string of car break-ins on their block, and they were victimized. Their car doors were left unlocked which made it easy for the thieves to get in. I'm pretty sure if the doors were locked that this highly opportunistic group would have just moved on to the next house.

The homeowners are not to blame for feeling safe, because feeling safe is not a bad thing. But leaving the car doors unlocked led to them becoming victims of crime and their feeling of safety to be taken away.

Don't Discount Yourself

Thinking your home is not nice enough to be robbed is false security. Thinking your neighborhood is safe because it is "nice" is false security. You cannot anticipate every reason someone would want to victimize you. Therefore, you cannot justify the notion that you will never be the victim of a crime.

Let's go back to the couple in the nice neighborhood. While their property may have been safe from larger-scale crime, it was not impervious to neighborhood kids being stupid and stealing from unlocked cars. That happens; it's just life. But you can take steps to secure yourself, your family, and your property to decrease the odds of being targeted for a crime.

Christmas Trash

On the first trash day after Christmas, criminals ride around all the nice neighborhoods to check out the trash cans. Here, criminals can see all of those discarded boxes and pinpoint the valuables in each home. People everywhere broadcast their new TVs and game consoles to the entire world without saying a word.

Criminals make a note of the house and add it to a hit list. Why are TVs and game consoles a high-value target? Items like these are easily carried out of a home and pawned without any trace. It's no wonder that nationally the recovery rate for electronics is only 4.9%.

It doesn't have to be Christmas to make your home a target. Last spring while on a walk in my neighborhood I spotted a home broadcasting their new toys to everyone. I had to walk around two large yard tool boxes tossed out beside the trash can.

This homeowner is telling everyone that there are great lawn tools to be taken from the garage. To make things worse, the garage door was open too. If you have large boxes, flatten them and stuff them inside the trash can or take them directly to the recycling center. Don't put a large advertisement in the yard for what you keep in your home.

Secure Dad Action Tip: Audit your trash on a weekly basis to make sure you're not inviting trouble. Think about the inadvertent signs you may be putting up in your yard.

Don't Advertise Your Children

Surprisingly, creating your own crime applies to people as well as possessions. Recently I discovered a new trend in yard signs and high school athletics. Parents who are very proud of their daughters making the varsity cheerleading squad will tell everyone how proud they are of their daughter's accomplishment. How do they do this? They create a sign and plant it in their yard that says "Your Town High School Cheerleader Lives Here" along with a picture.

No, I'm not kidding.

While I understand the pride parents have for their children's accomplishments, a yard sign is a disastrous idea. Young women are targeted for unwanted attention and sexual advances all the time. Don't draw more attention to your teenage daughters with a yard sign.

Never give away your daughter's location, school, and interests on a sign in your yard. It lets the bad guys know where your daughter will most likely be at night, where she goes to school, what her interests are, her potential schedule, and where her parents should be on Friday nights in the fall.

People don't put up yard signs telling everyone that they have expensive jewelry and electronics in their house. They know this can make their home a target for a burglary. Our children should be given the same consideration.

Secure Dad Action Tip: Don't make yard signs singling out your children's accomplishments. If you must buy the sign as part of the booster club, store in in the garage or let your kid have it in their room.

Don't Make it Easy

The same goes for giving a burglar an easy way into your home. Don't leave first-floor windows up or leave your garage door open when you leave. This is a crime waiting to happen. It's not enough to just keep the front door locked; you need to lock your windows and leave them closed whenever possible. If someone passes your home and sees an easy access point, they may be convinced to commit a crime because they see an easy way inside.

For example, on a warm spring day, you open a few windows in your home to let in the breeze. When it's time for you to meet a friend for lunch, you lock your doors and head out free as a bird. Your home will smell like a spring meadow when you return. Across the street a teenage neighbor sees you leave. He has recognized an opportunity.

Your young neighbor walks up beside your home and enters through a window not easily seen from the road. He dashes up the stairs, not to take your jewelry or electronics. He wants your prescriptions. The raid on your medicine cabinet is quick, and he's out the window with all the pills he needs. You just set up the perfect scene for a burglary.

Don't make it easy for someone to victimize you. In the above scenario, the chances of the teenage neighbor breaking into your home were nearly nonexistent. But when he saw you leave and that there was an easy way into your home, it was more than he could bear. Don't tempt people into robbing you.

This type of scenario can attract a first-time offender. Let's say the teenage neighbor from our scenario was only taking pills he got from his friends. Since you inadvertently created a situation that the teenager couldn't pass up, he's now a thief. You may not only create the crime; you may help create the criminal as well.

A Secure Routine

Discipline includes your daily commitment to having a secure routine like arming your alarm system, locking your doors, and making sure the garage door is closed. Installing home defense items is a great first step to being safer, but it takes a commitment to making sure they all function properly. You can have the best alarm system on the market, but if you never remember to arm it, it is useless.

You may be shocked to learn I didn't always make sure my home was safe. When I was in college, I was living alone in a transitioning neighborhood that was falling into the hands of drug dealers. I was rarely home thanks to two jobs, classes, and friends. My college apartment was frequently empty.

One day by accident I discovered that my back door leading to the porch was unlocked. I realized that the last time I used that door was three days ago. To make things worse, I lived in a duplex that backed up to a wooded area. Anyone could have come through that door!

It shook me to think that someone could have come in and taken all of my stuff while I was out. Even worse, I could have come home to someone waiting inside for me. Either way, I had made a terrible mistake, and I needed to correct it. That's when I began to develop a nightly safety sweep.

A nightly safety sweep is a secure routine to make sure your doors are locked, windows are locked, and your security system is armed before you go to bed. It's good to develop the habit of locking doors when you come and go, but before you settle down for the night, check to make sure everything is secure.

At a minimum every night you need to be checking to see if all of the exterior doors are locked with a deadbolt lock, all the windows are closed and locked, and that your security system is armed. As you go, you can add other things like turning on exterior lighting, brace doors with a door jammer, and closing the blinds.

If you've used your adversarial mindset, you know ways someone could break into your home. Add the elements you learned from this exercise to your nightly safety sweep as well.

Secure Dad Action Tip: Tonight, before you go to bed check to see if your home is secure. Then work to establish a routine of a nightly safety sweep.

Discipline plays a major role in keeping your home safe. From social media to the boxes in your trash can, you need to understand how your actions affect your home's safety. Don't create the opportunity for a crime, make sure you are proactive in keeping your home secure.

CHAPTER 4: LAYERED HOME DEFENSE STRATEGY: DETER

The most overlooked part of home security is deterrence. Far too many people think home security is passive, that no action is required until someone kicks in the door and the alarm goes off. What if we took simple steps to make sure an intruder never wanted to select your home as a target, and you don't have a nightmare scenario play out in your home.

The deterrence layer of this strategy is one that dissuades thieves from choosing to attack your home. Make your home unappealing to a thief, not because your home isn't valuable, but because of subtle warnings that you know what you're doing.

Speak to a potential thief in their own language: "My home isn't going to be your target." If you can demonstrate that your home should be difficult to break into, thieves will most likely move on. Thieves don't want to break into a home that is going to be well defended. Generally, they want easy targets.

Brighten Up Your Home

A thief's best asset is darkness. The lack of exterior lighting on a home creates pathways and hiding spots for criminals. Thieves know to look for dark homes with overgrown yards. If you have a bright yard, with trim shrubbery and light timers, a thief may doubt their ability to get into your

29

home quickly and quietly. You can make your home less of a target for thieves all the while appearing normal and well-maintained.

The first deterrent you need to employ for your home is exterior lighting. If a criminal can use the shadows to get across your driveway and alongside your home, then they have the upper hand in concealment. From a close distance, they can hide in the shrubs while they get a closer look at your front door and listen for any signs that you might be home.

From here it's a quick dash to the front door where the thief uses a kick-in attack to break it open. By adding exterior lighting and eliminating the cover of darkness, the thief is less likely to get close to your front door because he cannot risk being seen. He may dismiss your home as a target and move on.

Motion sensor lighting is a popular add-on for your home's security. These fixtures are mounted under the roofline of a home. They contain a motion sensor and two flood light bulbs that can be pointed in different directions. This is good because you want the light to hit driveways, corners, and gates, not your neighbor's bedroom window.

Another great advantage of a motion sensor light is that an intruder can't tell if the light is coming on because of an alert homeowner or a sensor. In a moment of panic the thief may wonder if he's tripped a sensor or worse, the homeowner has spotted him. At any rate, it's best for him to move on and get out of the light.

Floodlights pointed at your home also make a great deterrent. These lights are placed in the yard facing your home to eliminate darkness and also add a touch of class to your home's profile. Many people add floodlights in their yards as part of their Christmas decorating. I suggest keeping them up all year.

These lights can be solar, LED or have dusk-to-dawn capabilities. Combine this with pathway lights and motion sensor lighting for a well-rounded approach to security lighting. Your home should be brighter and can deter criminals while increasing your curb appeal.

Secure Dad Action Tip: Tonight, step outside to see where you can add exterior lighting to diminish any dark areas in your yard.

Dogs

Dogs make a great deterrent. They are security sirens with legs. They are also security sirens that poop. It's a tradeoff. You don't need a 90-pound junkyard dog to make your home safer. The one thing that all dogs can do is alert you to a developing situation, and criminals don't like that.

Dealing with a barking dog is not what a thief wants. However, you can't count solely on the dog's barking to deter a criminal. When your dog begins to act territorial and bark accordingly, you have to get up and look for what's causing their reaction. Most dogs won't do that for you.

The dog is an early warning system for you to act. You can opt for the junkyard dog that can fight to protect your property if you want, but any size pooch is good. So, if you've been looking for another reason to adopt a new furry friend, here you go.

Secure Dad Action Tip: If you have a dog, reward it when it barks at noises. While it may be annoying because you know it's barking at the mailman, encourage the dog to follow its instincts.

Don't Advertise Your Stuff

You may think that a way to avoid a break-in is a doormat that says: "We don't call 911" with a picture of an AR-15 on it. First, you do call 911. You must report a break-in. Even if you discharge your firearm at an attacker legally, you still have to call 911. Also, by posting a sign to this effect tells everyone that there is a gun in your home. Not good.

You should never advertise your belongings publicly. These types of signs simply tell thieves to get your guns they must wait until you're gone to break-in, rush to your safe in your master bedroom closet and to bring a grinder to cut through the flimsy side of the safe. You've developed their plan for them. Don't give away your possessions or defenses with a sign like this.

Alarm System Basics

A great deterrent is the presence of an alarm system at your home. But you need to understand exactly what an alarm system is designed to do. These systems are a passive network of sensors and cameras. They only work when something has tripped a sensor. In other words, they don't help you until something bad has happened.

If a burglar sneaks up and peeks into your window, the alarm doesn't sound. The same burglar tries the handle on your back door; the alarm doesn't sound. It's only when he kicks in the back door that the sensor on that door triggers an alarm. Hopefully, now the burglar realizes he's been caught, and is deterred from doing any further damage and flees your property.

I recommend you consider having an alarm system. We'll go over the basic requirements for an effective system. I use the phrase "alarm system" for a reason. Alarm system companies like to be called "security companies" because they say they provide security. That's debatable. While they do provide a process to alert you to a potential problem, home security is far more complicated than just an alarm system.

The first thing you need to note about these alarm systems is that they must be armed by you. Some have scheduling capabilities, but generally, it's you who has to activate your system. You can have the best system money can buy, but if you don't turn it on, it's useless. Make this part of your nightly safety sweep.

Don't get carried away with your alarm system either. While it may be fun to consider where to put sensors and cameras, at the end of the day you want to avoid making your home into a prison. The alarm system is there to alert your family to a problem. Don't make your family feel it's an authoritarian spy network.

Base Station

The base station is the command center of your security system. Generally, they can be a touchscreen tablet or a wall-mounted keypad. This is where you can arm and disarm your entire system, plus the siren is here too. That means it should be placed near to where you commonly enter the home.

The base station will likely have two-way communication so that you can be in contact with the alarm company in the event of a break-in. It may also have a panic button that will contact the monitoring company for you without making a call to them. Some panic buttons may be three separate buttons, one each for police, fire and medical emergency.

It's important to consider your home's internet connection when you're looking at a new system. Most likely your wireless alarm system will require its own router that is dedicated just for the operation of the system. Make sure you have a fast speed to support the extra stress an alarm system can have on your overall internet connection.

Secure Dad Action Tip: Remember to put up a generic security sign, not to advertise your specific alarm company. These signs are a deterrent all on their own.

Sensors

The first type of sensor your home alarm system should have is an entry sensor. These should be placed on every exterior door to your home. Even the door that leads to your attached garage if you have one. These sensors will send an alert when a door is opened. Depending on the mode, these sensors can trigger a full alarm or simple chime to let you know someone has entered your home.

Window sensors are another type of entry sensor that is placed on an individual window. Similar to the door sensors these are triggered when a window is opened. They help protect against someone who tries to unlock your window from the outside and raise it up to enter. The distance created when the window is open sets off the alarm.

Your budget may not allow you to put an entry sensor on every window. That can get expensive depending on how many windows you have. In this case, you can use a glass break sensor to cover your windows. These sensors use a microphone to alert the system to the sound pitch of breaking glass.

A motion sensor does exactly what you think; it detects motion in the given range of the sensor in a room. These can be great for covering large spaces or long rows of windows. These are smart sensors in that they can differentiate a 200-pound man from a 15-pound dog. These are good for open concept-homes.

Cameras

Cameras can be a fun addition to any alarm system, but they are costly as well. Not to mention they take up more bandwidth to push video across your Wi-Fi. The trick is finding the right balance for your home. You can have them inside, outside or both.

It's understandable that you might not want security cameras inside your home as it may feel like an invasion of privacy. If you put cameras inside, make sure that each member of your family is okay with them. If privacy and price are an obstacle try to have at least one exterior camera with night vision that can pick up the front of your home to see who is coming and going.

Siren

As noted before, your base station is likely where the siren is located. This should emit an ear-splitting sound when activated. While you are standing near your keypad trying to disarm the siren, you may think it's loud enough to wake the dead. However, try setting it off while you're in your bedroom.

When you set it off to test it in your room, does it sound loud enough to wake you? This is a real concern. You may think since you wake up from a smoke alarm you'll wake up for this too, but there are smoke alarms all over the home. There's only one siren with most systems.

If you can't hear it in bed, try getting a standalone siren to repeat any alarm you have and position it closer to where you sleep. You may even want to get a second base station to keep in your bedroom.

Secure Dad Action Tip: Test the siren on your alarm. Make sure it can be heard in all parts of your home. Plus, it can be a good refresher to remember what the alarm sounds like if you've not heard it in a while.

Alternate Access

It's wise to have an alternate way to arm and disarm your system. If you are coming home from the store, you can use a key fob or the smartphone app to disarm your system before you come inside. You may prefer a smartphone app to a key fob as it doesn't have to be a physical object on your keyring and can't be activated by accidental touch.

If your budget can take it, consider getting a panic button for your master bedroom. If you forget to set your alarm, or a bad guy gets around the sensors, you can manually trigger an alarm and alert the monitoring center that something is wrong with a standalone panic button. You may want to think about keeping it on your bedside table.

Monitoring

Just because you have 24/7 monitoring doesn't mean it replaces 911. The alarm system company isn't emergency dispatch for your local police department. They are a separate, standalone company.

If your alarm goes off while you are at home, don't wait for the alarm company to call you. There is a built-in delay for mistakes. When that alarm goes off, an adult should be assigned the responsibility of calling 911 as fast as possible. Use the alarm company as backup.

Code Words

If you have an alarm at your home, the alarm company will call to confirm the emergency. If there isn't an emergency, then the representative will ask you for a code word, so they know they are talking to the homeowner. This code word will have been set up when you purchased your system.

If you find yourself under duress, like a burglar is trying to manipulate you into getting them off the phone, then give the wrong code word. This way the alarm company will know something is wrong and notify the police. Likewise, you can type in a duress code on the keypad that will immediately notify the company that there is a problem.

There are many more cool gadgets that alarm companies have today. These have been the minimum requirements for an effective alarm system. If you don't have one, I strongly encourage you to do your own investigation into getting one for your home.

Secure Dad Action Tip: If you already have a system in place, audit it to make sure all the sensors are in working order.

CHAPTER 5: LAYERED HOME DEFENSE STRATEGY: FORTIFY

The third layer of our home defense strategy is fortification. The purpose of fortifying your home is to prevent or delay an intruder from entering your home by force. You want to make it hard for someone to get in, so they'll give up and move on. If they are determined to get in, then you'll want to make it take longer to breach your home, buying you time to prepare and call for help.

When making upgrades to your home's security keep in mind that fortifications don't need to repel a siege. Thieves strike quickly. If they don't get the results they want fast, then they are much more likely to abandon the attack. Fortifications should be made to last for several minutes, not hours.

While this may conjure up visions of a home with bars on the windows and a fence topped with razor wire, in reality, fortifications are much more practical. A fortified home does not need to look like a prison. No one wants to live in a prison. People want to find the balance between secure and inviting. Fortification can be done easily and won't detract from a home's curb appeal.

Fencing

The first line of any fortification is to put up a fence around the perimeter of your yard. If you live in a neighborhood, the homeowners association may have guidelines about where a fence can be placed and what it should look like. In my opinion, chain-link fences are only good for keeping in small dogs, and not much else. They're cheap, see-through and can be jumped over by any able-bodied person.

I suggest a wooden privacy fence. Wood privacy fences are six feet tall and repel most jumpers. It doesn't make sense to place a six-foot-tall fence around your front yard, that kills curb appeal. So, the better option may be to install a fence starting on the side of the home, extending around the back perimeter.

Make sure your HVAC units, power meter, and cable box are included inside the fence. This way the vital lifelines of your home can be protected. Make sure all gates are locked with a padlock. Your gates are important entryways just like your front door. I suggest you use a combination lock on each gate. That way you don't have the hassle of getting the key every time you mow the grass.

If you have small children in your home, then a combination lock may not be a good idea. If your kids have to flee your home in case of an emergency like a fire, then they might not be able to set the combination to escape.

That being the case you may want to consider using only a "D" ring from the hardware store to secure the gate. Get one that you would put on a chain, not one you'd put your keys on. This will only work if the locking portion of the handle is located on the inside of the gate.

Secure Dad Action Tip: If you already have a fence in place, make sure there is a combination padlock on each gate. Do your research on padlocks. They are not created the same. Some can be easily picked.

Moderation is Key

Fortifications need to be made in moderation. It's not wise to make a home completely impenetrable. While keeping thieves out is the top priority, there may come a time when first responders need to enter to provide assistance.

For instance, a man at home may suffer a heart attack. He's able to call 911 but unable to get to the door to let in the paramedics. In this case, the home needs to be breached to save his life. Likewise, firefighters need to be able to enter homes quickly to put out fires in homes when the owner is away. There is a balance to consider when fortifying a home.

Secure Dad Action Tip: Use your adversarial mindset again. How would a thief breach your home? Use this information to help strengthen your home's fortifications.

Chances are your home is ready to repel an attacker if you've followed the suggestions of this book so far. But your home has two important doors that can't be overlooked. To keep a home secure, don't forget to focus on the garage door and of course the front door.

The Garage Door

The garage is a vulnerable part of a home for reasons you've probably never thought about. You park your car, get out and go in the house. Or it's where you work out or store the boxes you never unpacked from moving. And you certainly don't think about your garage door as long as it is working. So why is the garage such a sensitive spot for a home?

The garage of any home contains many targets for thieves. In any given garage in America, there are tools, unlocked cars, sports and lawn equipment. Does someone really want a used blower? Yes, it can be pawned easily.

If the garage door is left open, especially when no one is home, everything inside is an easy take for a thief. Don't make your home a target for a crime. This is one of those crimes a homeowner can create unintentionally.

Keep it Secure

Keep the garage door closed. Yes, this is a simple as it sounds. A good percentage of homes in my neighborhood keep their doors open all day. Most people keep their front doors locked because they want to keep the bad guys out. The largest door to a home needs to be given the same consideration.

Many people leave their car doors unlocked in the garage. This makes a vehicle a target for theft as well. It can be relieved of all its valuables, not to mention that a skilled thief can hotwire the car and drive off.

Another reason to keep the garage door closed is to conceal that no one is home. An open garage door with no cars inside tells everyone that there are no adults home. Granted a teenager could be home for the day, but don't invite trouble for her.

When this sort of valuable information is given away, the likelihood of a home being targeted for a crime may increase. Don't give away any information to a crook. The less they can understand about a home the less likely it will become a target.

A garage can be used for storage space, or you may have more cars that can be parked inside. This means a car is parked in the driveway. Doing this leaves the garage remote, or clicker as I call it, exposed in the car. A burglar can break a car window and be inside the garage in under a minute. Store garage remotes in a console or glove box so that it can't be seen from the outside.

Secure Dad Action Tip: If you park a car in the driveway, make sure it is locked at all times.

Gaining Access

Once someone has access to the garage, bad things can happen. In the case of an attached garage, many people do not lock the door between the garage and their kitchen. This is a problem.

Once someone is in the garage, they can have easy access to the rest of the home if this door is left unlocked. Don't be taken by surprise when an intruder walks through the door unabated. Always lock the door leading from the garage into the home.

When someone gains access to a garage, they have a myriad of options to do more harm. Consider the contents of your garage for a moment. Do you store tools inside? Maybe a machete for yard work? A crowbar for the occasional odd job? When someone with bad intentions gets their hands on those types of items, they can be used against you. All a burglar needs do is close the garage door behind them, and they can work in secret to break into the rest of your home with your tools.

Hiding

Gaining access to the garage provides for another potential crime. Once inside a criminal can wait for a family member to come home and attack from a place considered "safe." Hidden away behind a few boxes or under an empty vehicle, an attacker can strike when it is least expected.

From here he can gain control not only to that family member but the rest of the family. Once a hostage is taken, compliance can be gained from the rest of the house. This is a bad scenario for any family.

Door Power

I've seen numerous blogs and infographics that encourage people to secure their garage by pulling the disconnect handle for the door. I think the idea is that you go on vacation and pull the emergency release handle to keep the motor from opening the door.

Thieves can use a programmable door opener that uses "rolling" codes to open garage doors. So, disengaging the garage door means the door can't be opened in a rolling code attack. Sounds good, right? Nope.

In reality what pulling the release handle does is put your garage door in "neutral." While the motor won't open the door, it can be manually opened from the outside. Disengaging the door from the motorized track can make it easier for a burglar to get in.

Instead, if you want to secure your garage from a rolling code attack, then you need to simply flip the breaker for the opener motor. That's it. This can keep the door down, and it can't be opened again electronically until the breaker is flipped back on. You need to plan to enter your home from another entry point as the garage door will be unresponsive until power is restored.

Secure Dad Action Tip: The next time you go on vacation consider flipping the breaker off for the garage door.

Fishing Attack

The internet is full of videos showing how a garage door can be hacked in 20 seconds with a coat hanger. The process is simple. A bad guy with a hanger bends it out and sticks the hook portion of the hanger above the middle of the garage door. Now he fishes around to find the switch that the emergency release handle is on. Hooking that switch and pulling should disengage the door from the motorized track, putting the door in neutral to opened manually from the outside.

This fishing attack can be foiled. The best way to secure the emergency release switch is with a ten-cent wire tie. From under the switch, wire tie it to the bracket that holds it onto the track. This should allow the door to function as normal but keep the emergency release switch from being pulled with a coat hanger.

Add a Lock

You might not know that garage doors can have keyed locks. For about $12 online you can order a lock system that can act like a deadbolt. This should only be used when away for an extended period as getting in and out of your car to manually unlock it every day would be beyond tedious.

There are electronic remote locks for garage doors, but unless you have a lot of extra cash, the $12 manual lock should secure your garage door if installed correctly. Guard the garage door as you would a front door. Keep it closed and secure all the time.

Secure Dad Action Tip: If you have an attached garage, go now and make sure the door is down. Then lock the door leading into the garage. Be sure to make a habit of this.

The Front Door

The front door of your home should look inviting to guests, not burglars. While it may seem shocking to think, most burglaries occur by gaining access through the front and back doors of a home.

While movies may fill audiences with ideas of high tech break-ins involving hacking and lasers, that's not usually the case. According to Nationwide Insurance, 34% of burglars gain access to a home through the front door making it the most common way a burglar enters a home.

I specifically discuss upgrades for the front door; many of these ideas can be applied to the back door as well. The back door accounts for 22% of break-in entry points. That means 56% of break-ins in America occur through a door.

Solid Doors

The first consideration to be given to bolstering a front door is the door itself. In a cost-saving move, most home builders use hollow, metal doors filled with fiberglass. Replace hollow doors with wooden ones. Wooden doors are usually solid and much heavier. This can be a costly upgrade.

Front doors with windows embedded in them should be avoided. While these decorative doors add a touch of class to an entryway, they are not very secure. The weakest point of this type of door is the glass itself. It can easily be smashed, and a burglar can reach inside and unlock the door quickly.

This also goes for windows around the door frame. A quick strike with a baseball bat can leave a hole large enough for a hand to fit through and unlock the door. Keep your door secure by removing the glass from around the doorway.

Secure Dad Action Tip: If your door has the hinges on the outside, which is uncommon, you need to have this fixed in the next 24 hours. Hinges need to be on the inside. Call a reputable handyman to come and fix the problem.

Get New Locks

If you have just purchased a home, the first thing that you need to do as the new owner is to replace all the door locks. While the former owners might have been nice people, you don't know who might have had a key to their home. Err on the side of caution and get new deadbolt locks and locking door knobs for a new home as soon as you close on it.

When purchasing a new lock set for your exterior doors, you have some options. You can purchase a single or double cylinder deadbolt. A single cylinder deadbolt is your normal lock with one exterior keyhole and a thumbturn (the lever your flip) on the interior. A double cylinder deadbolt has exterior and interior keyholes which means a key is necessary to unlock the deadbolt.

If you have decorative glass in your front door or glass around the door frame, a double cylinder deadbolt might be a good idea. This way if a burglar smashes a window and reaches around the door, there is no thumbturn for him to flip and open the door. He simply finds another keyhole.

Place the key for the interior cylinder nearby; do not keep the key in the cylinder. This defeats the advantage of the double cylinder deadbolt. I've had these locks before on doors with glass in them.

However, you must understand that double cylinder locks should not be used in a home with children. In the event of an emergency like a fire, children need to be able to get out of your home as easily as possible. Forcing a child to look for a key while your home is filling with smoke is a terrible idea. For that reason, only install single cylinder deadbolt locks in homes with children.

Door Reinforcer

Another way to fortify the front door is with a door reinforcer. This is a plate that surrounds your deadbolt and knob. These are easy to install and keep your door from splitting during a kick-in style attack. They can also add protection from an ice pick or a crowbar wedge attack.

These plates come in single, one lock, double deadbolt, and knob configurations. Being a homeowner, I suggest buying two individual plates to avoid any surprises at install time.

The Strike Plate

The deadbolt strike plate is the afterthought of your deadbolt door lock system. It's the part of the system that attaches to the door frame. It's usually installed last, or people just use the existing one when installing a new lock.

You can buy the best deadbolt lock on the market, but if deadbolt goes into a flimsy strike plate, it's not as effective. When a door is kicked in, it is usually the strike plate that fails, not the deadbolt lock.

Many companies now make a strike plate with a "strike box," or an enclosed chamber for the deadbolt to anchor inside. This enclosed area makes the strike plate much stronger and more resistant to being kicked in.

Also, in the strike box are usually two more holes for screws. So now you have four points to secure the strike plate to the door instead of the traditional two. This is a good upgrade for all the exterior doors of a home, not just the front door.

Not to be overlooked are the screws used to mount the strike plate. Most come with screws that are 1 inch or smaller. If the door is kicked in, the only thing holding the lock to the door are the 1-inch screws that can be torn out of the door frame. Instead, upgrade the screws to longer ones that will mount further inside the door frame, reinforcing the entire lock system. This is not an easy process; make sure your drill and bits are up to the challenge.

Secure Dad Action Tip: Check the strike plates on all of your exterior doors. Consider upgrading with an enclosed strike box installed with 2-inch screws.

A Storm Door

To potentially dissuade a front door break-in, consider a storm door. Having a sturdy storm door is a great way to make your front entryway more secure. A storm door with glass is much better than one that has a mesh screen. Make sure you install a glass storm door with a lock.

A storm door can keep the main doorknob, the deadbolt, and the door from being directly accessed by someone outside. This should make it more difficult for a potential thief to reach the front door to pick the lock or kick the door in. A storm door is an extra layer of defense that adds a look of class to the front of your home.

Additionally, if you have to open the front door to speak to someone, the main door can be opened while keeping the glass storm door closed and locked. This gives a barrier of safety while still being able to talk to the person. Be wary of someone who wants you to open the storm door or reaches to open the door themselves.

Most people who are trained to speak with customers on their doorstep are taught to back up while they make contact as not to appear aggressive. Anyone who wants entry to your home quickly should be considered a threat. If that is the case, close the main door, lock it and call the police.

Also note, companies make storm doors with shatterproof glass. This is an additional way to repel a very determined thief. This also can cause a potential safety problem. You do not want to make your front entryway impregnable, remember?

Fire, EMS, and police might have to access your home to save you from a variety of situations. Having shatterproof glass on a locked storm door can keep them from getting to you quickly. For that reason alone, I don't recommend you install shatterproof glass storm doors.

Door Viewers

To give you the upper hand in seeing who is at your front door, consider a $10 door viewer, or peephole as I called them growing up. These give you a secure view of your entryway while you stay behind the protection of your locked door. Not all front door attacks happen when residents are gone.

A common trick to get someone to open the door is to send a non-threatening woman to ask if anyone has seen her lost dog. While the resident is upset for this woman, an unseen man charges the door, knocking the resident down and gaining access to the home.

A door viewer can allow everyone close to the door to be seen. When shopping for a door viewer, make sure you get a wide angle one that can allow you to see all your entryway. Don't let someone press themselves against the wall without you seeing them.

I've heard many people say they are uncomfortable with the idea of a door viewer since someone standing outside can see when someone is looking out at them. From the outside, the light from the door view is eclipsed when someone looks out. This is noticeable to the person standing outside.

First, don't be concerned with someone else's feelings over your safety. Don't let politeness get you killed. This is your home and your safety. Do not feel bad for being cautious about your own safety.

Second, a door viewer cover can help this problem. These covers hang over the door viewer like a pendulum on the inside of the door. They block the light coming from inside the home so the person on the outside should not notice a change in light when the cover is moved out of the way to look outside. Both a door viewer and door viewer cover are easy to install.

Smart Door Bells

If you are a tech-savvy person, then you may want a smart door viewer/doorbell combo. There are a variety of camera door viewers/doorbells that can allow you to see outside via a Wi-Fi connection. Users can see who is outside their door when they are away from home. Some come with software that allows not only video recording but two-way audio too.

An advantage is that a smartphone can be notified when the doorbell is pressed. This would allow you to see and speak to the person at your door while you are not home. This would give the illusion you are home. Why is this important?

I've seen a few interviews with convicted felons who are serving time in prison for burglary. Many of them say they knock on the front door to see if anyone is home. If no one responds, then they kick in the front door. If someone does respond, they make up an excuse for having the wrong house.

If that happens to you, ask the person a few questions to see if they stumble to make up a story on the spot. Being able to talk to someone on your porch from another location could deter a break in.

Smart Locks

You may have considered a smart lock for your front door. A smart lock is a Wi-Fi or Bluetooth enabled deadbolt that can lock and unlock using an app. These are offered by alarm companies and can be purchased individually.

While this style of lock is cool, it has its drawbacks. I can't trust that it couldn't be hacked. If you want to control multiple people accessing your home, install a keypad lock that requires a user be at the door to open it.

Door Jammers

An easy way to fortify your entry doors is to add a layer of resistance with a door jammer. Door jammers do not require any permanent installation, which makes them a perfect solution for apartments. The drawback is that they must be set up every night.

The typical door jammer is a metal rod with a metal fork to go under the doorknob and rubber foot that goes onto a hardwood floor. Setup is quick and simple. Tuck the forked end under the doorknob and brace against a hardwood or laminate floor on the interior of your home. This additional reinforcement of an entry door gives great resistance to a kick-in style attack. I am a fan of the BuddyBar Door Jammer.

Bump Key Attacks

Some criminals have the skills to bypass all sorts of locks by picking them. They have a unique set of skills that allow them to open a lock with specific tools and practice. But now those skills aren't necessary when anyone can buy a bump key. No really, you can buy them on Amazon and learn how to use them on YouTube.

A bump key is a generic key with teeth. They look like any other key. On closer inspection, you'll see that all of the teeth look the same and are placed uniformly apart for the length of the key. These keys are engineered to open specific brands of locks. When inserted the user "bumps" or hits the key with a screwdriver as they turn. Within a few bumps most any deadbolt can be opened.

Don't worry—we have a way to combat bump key attacks. As mentioned before, a door jammer will keep the door from being opened even if the lock is bypassed. It should stay braced under the doorknob against the floor. You can also use a flip guard to keep your deadbolt from turning.

A flip guard attaches to the interior side of the deadbolt lock. The arm flips down over the thumb turn (the lever your flip) and physically keeps it from turning to unlock the deadbolt. That will make it nearly impossible for the lock to be turned to open. The lock can only be opened when the flip guard is moved back up.

A word of caution though. Since a flip guard is so effective, it can only be opened from the inside. If you are locked out, you may have to break through the door or break a window to get into your house. Weigh the options before you install one. Like bump keys, they can also be purchased on Amazon.

While the above information may seem overwhelming all at once, if you take it one portion at a time—one step at a time—you'll see how easy it is to fortify your home. These fortifications will strengthen your home and will keep it looking inviting.

CHAPTER 6: LAYERED HOME DEFENSE STRATEGY: DEFEND

So far in our layered home defense strategy, we've covered: discipline, deter, and fortify. These are the outer three layers of the plan. They are designed to keep people out of your home and buy time to respond to any threat. Now is when we examine the last layer of the home defense strategy, defend.

A family protection plan for your home, or home invasion plan, is when you consider how you plan to respond to an intruder in your home. Just like a fire escape plan, you must consider how many people live in your home, who needs help to act, consider where the danger is coming from, and how you can protect your family until help arrives.

The layered home defense strategy is to keep you from reaching the point where you must defend your family from an attacker in your home. If we correctly execute a layered home defense strategy, then the chances of a physical confrontation with an intruder can be greatly reduced. If you must enact the defend portion of this strategy that means all of the other layers have failed, and you are in a serious situation.

Defending your home from a potentially armed intruder is a scary thought. The advantage of a layered home defense strategy is deterring a break-in from ever occurring. However, this may not be enough to repel determined predators.

Sometimes the intent of a criminal outweighs the concern of being caught. Or the attacker could be under the influence of alcohol or drugs and is not behaving rationally at all. Regardless, the result is your home coming under attack.

Now it is time to act. It is time to defend.

Defending

When faced with a physical defense situation in the home, you need to decide what you are prepared to do to fight for your family. This decision needs to be reached today, not in the heat of the moment. Are you prepared to severely injure someone to protect your family? Have you decided whether you are willing to inflict a fatal injury on someone to defend yourself and your family? You need to know the answers to these questions.

No one wants to kill an intruder. That's why we have a layered home defense strategy, an alarm system, and locks on our doors. We want to be left alone to live our lives in peace. We are not aggressors; we are protectors. We are going to do everything we can to avoid a physical encounter with an intruder. We are not inviting trouble. We are declaring our boundaries, and if they are breached, we will respond accordingly.

There are times when calm, well-mannered people have to stand up and fight for their lives and the lives of their loved ones. Decide in advance what actions you are willing to take to secure your family so when your heart is racing, and your senses are diminished you can know how to respond.

Secure Dad Action Tip: Take time today to deliberate what you are willing to do to protect yourself and your family. This is an intense subject that cannot be taken lightly. Give it careful consideration.

Home Defense Tools

Many people think the only home defense tool is a firearm, but there are many different options for you to consider. If you own a firearm, don't skip this part. Choosing a defensive tool for home defense is a unique process as it depends on you, your mindset, your family, your home, and your layered home defense strategy. I realize that firearm ownership isn't for everyone, so that's why we'll look at a variety of options for home defense tools.

I Own a Gun. So, I'm Good, Right?

People buy firearms for a variety of reasons: to have a hobby, go hunting, participate in a competition, and, of course, home and personal defense. I have met men and women, young and old that think since they have a gun in a drawer of their nightstand, their home is safe. It's dangerously naïve to think your home is completely safe just because you have a gun in a drawer of your nightstand.

The issue of home security is much more complex than a single defensive tool. I maintain that there is no "one size fits all" solution to home security. That also means there isn't a singular solution for home security either – including firearms.

People want to know if owning a firearm makes their home safer. Certainly, having one for self-defense can stop or deter an intruder. But then people worry about storing it safely or the trigger being pulled accidentally. So, my answer to the question is this: it depends.

Does my answer depend on the crime rate of the area? Does it depend on the type of firearm? No, the answer is much simpler. Whether or not a firearm makes a home safer is directly dependent on the competency of the firearm owner.

If the owner is trained to use the firearm, locks it up when it is not in use, and obeys the rules of gun safety, then a home can be made safer with a firearm for protection. If the owner fails to know how to use it, has never trained with it, stores it improperly, and has no clue what the rules of gun safety are, then the home is actually less safe.

I highly recommend to everyone who owns a firearm that you get hands-on training on how to use it from a certified instructor in your state. Also, be sure you are familiar with any state and local laws regarding firearm use and self-defense. While books, YouTube, and internet articles are good resources to teach concepts of defensive firearm principles, nothing beats hands-on training. Plus, you'll have a good time doing it.

Whether or not firearm ownership is for you, let's discuss some other home defense tool options.

Secure Dad Action Tip: All firearms are to be locked up until they are needed. Then, only people who know how to use the firearm are to have access to it. Children should never have access to a gun. Ever.

Tasers

Tasers utilize dart-tipped electric wires that can be deployed in close quarters. Others rely on being close enough to jab electrical prongs into the body of an attacker. Some have both features. Tasers create space, are generally considered less lethal, and pose little threat to bystanders.

Some tasers can be used more than once. They're loaded with cartridges that can be fired once or twice. The cost of replacement cartridges is high, so practice can be expensive. Also, know that being shot with a taser does not mean instant incapacitation. I've seen plenty of police videos where suspects weren't phased by them. While tasers are less effective than firearms when it comes to stopping power, they are much better than our next defensive tool, pepper spray.

Pepper Spray

Many people choose to arm themselves with pepper spray for personal defense. When used correctly, pepper spray can deter even the most dogged attacker. A word of warning though about using pepper spray indoors – don't do it unless you have no alternative.

What most people don't realize is that while the pepper spray stream is concentrated, there is still overspray. Plus, the spray isn't absorbed by its target, creating blowback and it can fill the surrounding air with remnant spray. It is not ideal for indoor use as the remnant can float in the air and affect others, including the people you're trying to protect.

Worst of all, the spray can get into your home's HVAC system and distribute the potency throughout every room in your home. (I know of a Waffle House that was evacuated for this reason.) I suggest that you not use pepper spray as a home defense tool.

Baseball Bat

The classic choice of sitcom fathers everywhere is the baseball bat for home defense. Chances are you have a bat in your home already and can quietly place one where you can get to it quickly. Your kids may not understand that it's a defensive tool and won't think twice about it being under your bed or in a closet.

If you are going to use a bat as a weapon, know that it requires some distance to strike your attacker. If the attacker gets within arm's reach, the advantage of the bat is negated. You won't have enough room to swing. Keeping your distance is a must with a bat. A blow to the head from a bat is devastating to a person, and it may cause serious injury or death. Make sure you know what you're willing to do to protect your family.

Empty Hand Skills

The term "empty hand skills" is a fancy way of saying martial arts and self-defense training. I highly recommend this type of training, even if you are proficient with another home defense tool. With empty hand skills, your hands are the defensive tools. There isn't anything to hide in the home or anything a child could stumble upon and hurt themselves with.

I've studied basic Krav Maga for self-defense, and it was a worthwhile endeavor. I discovered much about myself, what I was good at, and what I wasn't so good at. It opened my eyes to how fast violence can strike and how out of hand a situation can become if you are not prepared. By no means am I an expert or proficient enough to teach others, but I am better prepared to defend myself and my family.

When I considered defense training, I was nervous about starting. Take it from me, don't be afraid to pick up the phone and call an instructor to schedule a class. These instructors live to teach others their discipline for competition, exercise, and self-defense. Martial arts and self-defense instructors can be some of the kindest people you'll ever meet.

Knowing some martial arts or self-defense can make you safer at home and while in public. No metal detector can remove your empty hand skills; they are always with you.

Serious Consequences

We've discussed a variety of self-defense tools here. Some are considered "less lethal," some aren't. Defending yourself and your family may have significant consequences. There is a chance you may kill an attacker while defending your home with any defense tool. That's why it's so important to understand what you are willing, and not willing to do to keep yourself and your family safe.

It all comes down to your mindset. What are you prepared to do to protect your family? The tool you use to defend your home should only be used when all the other aspects of your layered defense strategy fail. If you must use it, that means it's a bad day, and your worst-case scenario is coming true. That being the case, consider a defensive tool that can stop an attacker quickly and at a distance. Regardless of what you choose, keep in mind that you are the weapon, and the firearm/taser/bat is simply a tool.

Defending with a Family Protection Plan

When all the layers of discipline, deter and fortify have failed, and an intruder is in your home, you should never go out and search for a bad guy. If you go looking for trouble, you're going to find it. What you need to do is fall back to a place where you know you can mount a substantial defense. Such a place is called a safe room.

Safe Room

A safe room is a place where your family needs to assemble in case of an invasion. If kids are old enough, they can get there on their own. Smaller children, elderly adults, and those with special needs should be assigned a responsible person to get them to the room as quickly as possible.

Your safe room needs at minimum a telephone, windows facing the street, and a limited number of doors. It also needs to be accessible to every member of the family. If all family members sleep on the second floor, then the safe room needs to be on the second floor as well. This room also needs to be used in the event of a daytime break-in. Gathering in the safe room should be fast and simple.

Please note that getting to your safe room may not be possible. Discretion is necessary. For instance, your family is at the dinner table at the back of the home. An intruder enters through an open front window. He is between you and your safe room. At this point, it would be better for your family to exit the house and flee to a neighbor's home to call for help.

Assembling

When your family is assembling in the safe room, try to make an attempt to end the situation by commanding that the intruder leave. Who knows, they just might leave! Remember, we want to avoid a conflict. While this may sound odd, a police officer, or a lawyer, may ask you if you made any effort to notify the intruder to leave your home. If asked, it would be useful to say that you did.

If you have a self-defense tool like a firearm, make sure it is not a danger to your family. If you're not comfortable physically defending yourself, or unable to do so, that is good to know. This will be a scary time, and you need to act in accordance with what you feel you can do. Otherwise, you might get yourself hurt.

The door to your safe room needs to be barricaded as quickly as possible. Interior doors are often lightweight and hollow. They can be kicked in easier than exterior doors. By fortifying the door with dresser, bookshelf or a mattress, you can slow down and even deter an intruder. Do not use your body to barricade the door. As stated before, interior doors are hollow and won't stop a bullet from penetrating it. Block the door with something heavy and then get away from it.

Calling for Help

A responsible person should be assigned to call 911 as soon as you enter the room and the door has been barricaded. This task should be assigned to an adult or teenager who can speak under pressure.

I suggest you keep a landline phone just for this type of an emergency. Most 911 call centers can identify the address of your landline quickly. It can be hit or miss with a cell phone. Some 911 call centers can even take text messaging. However, a phone call from a landline should be faster than a text conversation. Only use texting if you are hiding.

If you own an alarm system, then a representative may be calling to confirm the emergency. If you are assembled and the call has not come, then go ahead a call 911. Do not wait for the alarm company.

When you answer the alarm company call, tell them that you need help and to send the police. At this point, they may ask you to stay on the line. Don't let this hinder you from executing the rest of your family protection plan. You can always put the phone down without hanging up.

Escaping

If you live in a single-story home, then your safe room needs to include functioning windows, so that you can slip out in a hurry. Run to the neighbor's house or another pre-planned rally point. When you hear the police approaching, flag them down and tell them your situation.

By escaping your home, police know that your family is safely outside. Now they know that anyone they encounter inside is a threat. This is an easier situation to deal with for first responders and a safer option for your family.

A quick escape may not be possible. If your safe room is on the second floor, use the window facing the street to call for help and communicate with first responders who are arriving after your emergency call. Make sure the police know where your family members are located so they can easily identify the intruder. Make it as easy as you can for the police to find the bad guy.

You can practice this with your family just like you would a fire drill. In the event of an emergency, everyone knows where to go. By having a plan and a safe room, you're telling everyone – the intruder and the police – that you are doing everything you can to protect your family.

Secure Dad Action Tip: Walk through your home and determine the best location for your family safe room. Also, see what you can use to barricade the door and make sure the windows are in working order.

Home Invasion Kit

A home invasion kit should be a bag or box located in your safe room. This kit should only be used if there is a home invasion emergency. The kit should include items you need to help you when seconds count.

The first item in your home invasion kit is a spare key. A great way to let police access your home during a break-in is to keep a spare key to the front door with a light up keychain in your safe room. This way someone inside can toss the key out the open window to the police so they can enter the house quickly.

The light on they keychain should make it easy for an officer to spot it, saving precious time. If you have more than one front door, like a storm door, put that key on the ring as well. Then color code the keys with labels so the responding officer can quickly determine which key is for which door.

You also need a small folding knife. The knife can be used to cut any window screen that may prohibit someone from throwing the keys down to your lawn. It can also be used as a defensive tool if necessary. Use a folding knife instead of a fixed bladed one so that when you're frantically reaching inside the kit, you won't cut yourself. If you have small children in the home, store the home invasion kit where little hands cannot access it.

A flashlight should also be in the kit. Consider getting an LED super bright light. This can temporarily blind an attacker if your safe room door is breached. You'll also be able to see more details of the attacker for identification later. Also, the flashlight can be used to flag down first responders from the window.

Your home invasion kit needs to include a signal horn. The horn can be sounded to attract the attention of neighbors and first responders. It may also scare off the intruders. When you need to use the horn, extend your arm out the window and sound it outside your home to preserve as much of your hearing as you can. You can find these small compressed air horns online or in boating stores.

Secure Dad Action Tip: Find a bag or box to start your home invasion kit.

When the Police Arrive

Just because the police have arrived doesn't mean the danger is immediately over. The key to staying safe once law enforcement has arrived is communication. Tell them you're throwing down a key. Tell them all of your family is in your safe room. Then listen for any further instructions.

At this point, you may want to leave the safe room to assist the police by pointing out the intruders to the waiting officers. Do not leave the safe room until the police get you, even if there is an injury. Stay put and let the officers do their jobs. Your job is to protect your family in the safe room.

Once you are cleared to leave the safe room, continue that good communication. If someone is hurt, you may need an ambulance. If you've used a self-defense tool to defend your home, secure it so that there isn't an accident. Don't walk toward a police officer with something that could be considered a weapon. Remember they are just as jumpy as you are.

You may discover that under the stress of the situation that you may not remember the events in order. If this is the case, ask for a few moments to be with your family and make sure they are physically and emotionally okay. Once the officers know the intruder is gone, or hopefully handcuffed in a patrol car, things should become more casual.

Physical Defense

The last thing you ever want to have to do in the event of a home invasion is to physically defend yourself. The layered home defense strategy is designed to deter criminals from targeting your home in the first place and then keeping them away from your family if they enter the home. The safe room is the final plan of protection. If the safe room is breached, then you are left with a physical defense situation.

While I can't predict your exact home defense situation, you can reasonably assume that if an intruder breaches your safe room, then they are intent on hurting you. You may not know why, and you don't have time to figure it out. Now you have to fight for yourself and your family.

This is when your decision you reached days, weeks, months, or years ago about what you're willing to do to keep your family safe comes into play. This is where everything you've trained for comes together. Your self-defense tool, training, and mental preparedness now have to stop the threat.

This is going to be ugly. It is going to be uncivil. It is going to be frightening.

Give yourself permission to do what is necessary to save your life and protect your family. I don't think you can be fully ready for it, but you can be prepared. You'll be prepared because of your mindset, your hands-on training, and your internal desire to protect the ones you love most. When that threat comes through the safe room door, be ready to stop it. Let your attacker(s) know that the most dangerous place in the world is between them and your family.

Secure Dad Action Tip: Imagine the moment when all of your defenses have failed to repel your intruder(s). What does that look like? Where are you? Where is your family? Have you done any hands-on training? Do you have a defensive tool? The sooner you know the answers to these questions, the better off your family should be.

CHAPTER 7: PUTTING THE PLAN INTO ACTION

We've been over a lot of new, thought-provoking information. Let's break a layered home defense down into a scenario of what might happen if someone tries to invade a home while a family is sleeping. This will be based on a family of four, two adults and two children, living in a two-story home.

On a summer night, you are getting ready for bed. The sun's down, and your porch light comes on automatically as it should. You set your alarm and check your doors as you always do. Everything seems in order.

After several hours of sleeping, you hear a loud thud. You awaken and listen harder to pinpoint where the sound came from. There's another loud thud. Now it's clear someone is hitting your back door. Your dog now begins to bark and growl downstairs.

You tell your startled wife to call 911 as you spring out of bed. Both of you are not wasting time wondering why this is happening or what the person at the door wants; you are executing your family protection plan.

As you enter the main hall outside of all of the bedrooms, you see your 10-year-old son standing in his doorway. He's panicked. You put two hands on him and push him in the direction of your master bedroom as that is your safe room. While your son was aware of what to do in the event of an emergency, he still needed help getting to the safe room. There is another loud thud and a cracking sound.

You dash into your 6-year-old daughter's room. Somehow, she is still asleep. In the dark, you search around the tangled blankets and stuffed animals and pick her up. There is a final bang from the back door, and your alarm siren triggers its ear-splitting sound. The intruder is now inside.

Your daughter is somehow still sleeping in your arms as you enter your safe room. Your wife has already been on the phone with 911 for about a minute. She's communicated the situation and your address. She's sheltering your son in the corner near a window. You place your daughter temporarily on the bed as you turn to close and lock your bedroom door. Before closing and locking the door, you yell:

"Get out of my home!!! Leave now!!!"

As you secure the door, the siren continues to wail. Your wife now has both children sheltered in the corner still on the phone with 911. You know it's now time to barricade the door. You have planned to push a bookcase in front of the bedroom door. The bookcase is too heavy to push, so you tip it over, and it falls in front the door with a loud bang. Books and picture frames are all over the floor. The fallen bookcase is completely blocking the lower portion of the door, so it can't open.

Your wife is opening the window. She can now communicate and flag down any responding law enforcement officers. She scrambles to open a small bag that is your home invasion kit while still on the phone. She gets out the small folding knife and cuts a hole in the window screen. She can now toss keys out of the window and use the signal horn. You take this time to grab your shotgun in your fast access safe.

For the moment you can't hear the intruder. The alarm is still blaring, and the dog is barking downstairs. Your heartbeat is pounding in your ears. You can hear your wife talking on the phone, but you can't make out what she's saying. Is the intruder gone? Why aren't the police here yet? How long has it been? Is anyone hurt? Do I need to check the house? Is it over?

BAM!

Your thoughts are brought sharply into focus as the intruder has reached your safe room door. He's trying the handle and pounding on the interior door. At this point, it is safe to assume that this intruder means you harm or is high on some sort of narcotics. He's had plenty of notification to leave and has chosen not to go.

He tries again to break down the door. You shoulder up your shotgun. You don't want to shoot anyone, but you're prepared to defend your family. Firing through the door would be a bad idea. If he breaches the door, you know you might be forced to shoot.

At the window, your wife sounds the signal horn and she's yelling out of the window. Your safe room is filled with flashing blue lights. Your focus was so concentrated on the door, you couldn't hear the approaching police sirens. Your wife has flagged down the responding officers with the air horn out of the window.

Your wife tells them there's an intruder in the house, your family is barricaded in your safe room and that you are armed. She tosses down your spare front door key on a lighted keychain. The police instruct her to keep everyone in place until they get you. The officers begin their search for the intruder.

The intruder has been quiet for the last few seconds. He's stopped pounding on the door. From downstairs, you can hear muffled voices yelling. You take the shotgun off of your shoulder. Quickly you look back at your family; they seem to be okay. Shaken up, but okay.

After a few moments, more police arrive. Not knowing what to do, you hold your position at the door. Your wife calls you to the window to see the police escorting a man in handcuffs to a patrol car. They got him.

You did your job. The police did theirs.

Relieved, you place the shotgun back in the safe and return to hug your family. There's a polite knock at the door as an officer tells you the threat is over. It's safe to come out. Your family protection plan was executed, and because of that, your family is safe.

Breaking it Down

In the above scenario, we see that your family protection plan is a team effort. Everyone knew their part of the plan. Except for the daughter who slept through the first part of the invasion. You can't assume that everyone is going to react accordingly. Even the 10-year-old son knew what to do, but he hesitated because he was understandably scared.

The adults knew their roles and very little talking occurred between the two. There was a list of actions each one needed to complete, and they did it. The husband, you in the scenario, gathered the children, told the intruder to leave, barricaded the door and gathered a defensive tool ready to fight if necessary. The wife called 911, sheltered the children, flagged down the police and tossed the spare key out.

Upon hearing a siren, a dog barking and people shouting inside the home, many thieves would abandon their plan and flee. The scene continued with a worst-case scenario so that we can walk through all the steps of a family defense plan. Even if you think the intruder is gone, continue to barricade yourself inside your safe room until the police arrive and tell you it's safe to come out.

Some readers may disagree about the timing of retrieving the home defense tool, the shotgun. In this scenario, the husband was going to have to dig around in his daughter's bed to retrieve her. Doing that while holding a firearm would be dangerous and could have terrible unintended consequences. That's why the home defense tool wasn't produced until everyone was in the safe room. You may feel differently. That's why you are in charge of your family protection plan.

This was only a teaching scenario. If you have a home invasion while you're at home sleeping, it may not look anything like what I've scripted. That's why you need to take the information given here and do more research on your own to make informed decisions for your family protection plan.

This is a lot to consider. As I've said, there is no "one size fits all" solution to home security and family protection. I cannot predict your specific threat you may face. You cannot either. That is why it's wise to be prepared for a variety of possibilities. That is why a layered home defense strategy makes sense. It keeps out a variety of threats. Do everything you can to keep intruders from targeting you. Then do everything you can to keep them out.

CHAPTER 8: A SECURE LIFE

The Secure Dad empowers fathers to lead safer, more secure families giving them the freedom to enjoy the blessings of life. This is accomplished when we realize that we can be the victim of a crime and change our mindset and validate our intuition. We need to develop and expand a secure mindset so that when any emergency arises, we are prepared to protect and aid our loved ones.

Having a secure mindset isn't a life of paranoia. I don't go to bed at night in fear of someone kicking in the door. I have a plan to deal with that, and my plan gives me the confidence I need to respond to that situation when necessary. Paranoia is being fearful of something you can't predict or control. A secure mindset is being prepared to respond swiftly when necessary.

Having a secure mindset is being prepared and confident you can minimize the event of a threat. With this way of thinking, you can be sure of your ability to protect your family and free your mind to enjoy life. A fearful man hides his family at home. A secure man protects his family as they enjoy their lives.

Now that you've had the chance to read this book, I hope you start to take steps to embrace a secure mindset. When you do, you can become safer than you were before. The information included here is meant to get you thinking about how you can make your family more secure while enjoying life.

Start making your home safer today by implementing what you've learned. Think about how you can apply the layered home defense strategy to your home. Check your deadbolts to make sure they extend all the way to their locking positions. Install dusk-to-dawn light bulbs to deter intruders. Keep your travel plans off of social media. These are all simple things that can be done today to immediately make your family safer.

Because you were interested in reading this book, I'm going to give you my Basic Home Security Checklist for free. This list covers the basics you need to cover to start to make your home more secure. Go to www.thesecuredad.com/checklist-for-readers.

As I have said before, there is not a "one size fits all" approach to your family's safety and home security, including this book. There are other great books, online courses, and training you can receive to increase your awareness and skills. Also, continue to check in on TheSecureDad.com as I update the site frequently with relevant information for you to use to keep your family safe.

The purpose of this book has been to provide families with the information they need to make more informed decisions about their personal safety. I can't predict every dangerous situation in which you may potentially find yourself. Ultimately it will be up to you to defend yourself and your family. If you must take action, make sure you are ready.

DID YOU ENJOY THIS BOOK?

I hope that you enjoyed reading this book. More so, I hope you take this information and use it to make more informed decisions about your family's safety. If you have enjoyed it, would you please consider taking a moment to review this book on Amazon?

It will only take a moment, and your review may help a family like yours begin to live a safer life today.

God bless you and your family as you work to lead a happier, more secure, lifestyle.

Andy Murphy
The Secure Dad

APPENDIX: HOW TO SECURE YOUR HOME WHILE ON VACATION

A family vacation is always something to look forward to. You want to be relaxing, trying new things and enjoying being with your family. But for some, being on vacation is all they think about, with little thought given to securing their home while they are gone.

You don't want to return home from a trip of a lifetime to a ransacked house. Making sure that your home is secure while you are gone is as important as making your travel plans. The good news is that there are some simple steps you can take to make your house look occupied and therefore less attractive to a burglar.

Pack Discreetly

We all hate packing. There's a lot of guesswork in making sure you have everything you need. Then you must lug all the luggage to the car and cram everything in while not destroying your belongings. It's a process.

Once I passed my neighbor's home to find their van sitting in the middle of the driveway with all the doors open. Every member of the family was furiously running around throwing in bags and beach chairs. My first thought was that there must be hornets inside the car and they were fleeing for their safety. It was total chaos!

Then I realized this was how they were packing for vacation. An adult would grab a large bag and throw it in the back while the teenagers tossed backpacks and snacks in the middle. It was the oddest sight not because it was so disorganized, but because they were letting everyone around know that they were leaving their house in a matter of minutes and would be gone for a while.

When you leave your home to go on vacation, it shouldn't look any different than a trip to the store. If you have a garage, pack your car with the door down so that no one can see you packing. If you must pack in the driveway, or in an apartment parking lot, stage all of your luggage inside and bring out a piece at a time and load it. Don't put everything out for everyone to see. Don't tip off anyone that you're about to leave your home for an extended time.

Light Timers

For as long as I can remember my father always used light timers when we went on vacation. As he explained to me, a house that is dark inside lets people know you are not home. When you are home, the lights are on. Maintaining the appearance of being home can deter a thief from targeting your home.

My father used timers that were these thick boxes that looked to be a cross between an egg timer and a sundial. Fortunately, technology has advanced for lighting timers. Now we have Wi-Fi controlled smart timers. I have always been impressed with WEMO Wi-Fi enabled smart products. WeMo works with a smartphone app and with the Amazon Echo.

Smart plugs can be controlled from a computer or smartphone if you have Wi-Fi in your home. Wi-Fi enabled smart plugs fit into a three-pronged outlet in your home. From here you can plug a lamp into the smart plug and set the timer on the respective smartphone app. Be aware that a single lamp's light will not produce the same brightness that you may normally use on a typical night.

That being the case you can upgrade the bulb in the lamp to a higher wattage. Also, consider removing the lampshade and moving it closer to your window to try and recreate a normal lighting situation for that room.

If that sounds too complicated, you can have an electrician install a smart Wi-Fi switch on your overhead lighting. This functions like the plug so that you can set a timer in the app, but it also acts as an everyday switch for the light fixture. Plus, you can have fun turning on and off the lights from the comfort of your couch. Who doesn't want that?

Timing is everything with timers. When using lighting timers, we're not trying to create a scene like a rave in your living room. You simply want to make your home look normal. If the lights come on in the living room at 6:00 am and go off at 7:30 am when you go to work, then set that pattern up. Then program them to simulate you returning home at 5:30 pm and going off at your normal 11:30 pm schedule.

Unlike the old days where timers turned on and off at a set time, smart plugs can turn on and off at a range of times. This eliminates being able to predict the exact moment a light turns off aiding in the illusion that someone is in the home.

Securing Entry Ways

Of course, you will lock your doors when you leave to go on vacation, right? But when was the last time you checked your windows? Before you set out on your grand tour, make sure to physically check all of your windows, doors, and gates to make sure they are locked. You may want to take further precaution on your main doorways by fortifying them with a door jammer.

Set Your Alarm

You can have the best alarm system money can buy, but unless it's used correctly – it's worthless. Lots of people buy alarms and think they'll run themselves. That's not entirely true. There are programmable automated options for some systems, but you have to set them up.

Most alarms have three basic modes, home, away, and night. When you leave for work typically away mode is used because it allows you to trip a sensor, meaning you open a door, and have 30 seconds to disarm the system. When you leave for vacation, you might think this is the best idea, but let's consider another option.

While away on vacation I suggest you set your alarm to night mode. This is because on most alarm systems night mode immediately sets off an alarm when a sensor is triggered. That means as soon as a door, window or motion sensor is tripped it sounds the alarm and notifies the monitoring company.

If you choose away mode while gone, then burglars have up to 30 seconds to smash and grab whatever they can before the alarm sounds and the monitoring company is notified. It's best to have the alarm sound as soon as possible to alert neighbors and those monitoring your home's system.

Property Check

One of the tools that I use when my family travels is to call and request a property check by the police. A property check is when an officer comes to your home and inspects your property for anything unusual. It's discreet and usually costs you nothing.

To set one up, simply call the main line for your local police department or sheriff's office. Do not call 911 as this is not an emergency. When asked, tell them that you are calling to request a property check of your home while you're on vacation. Police departments get these requests every day.

Hopefully, they will ask you a few questions beyond the basic contact information. You'll have to tell them when you'll be gone, if anyone should be at the residence while you're away, and if any vehicles should be parked outside. They may even give you a few suggestions like using light timers and making sure your mail is held while you're gone.

From here an officer should check your residence as part of their shift while you are away. If anything is found amiss during the officer's check, he can act immediately. Don't expect more than one property check during your vacation unless you request it. This is a valuable service that should only take 10 minutes to set up.

The Mailbox

The biggest giveaway for an unoccupied home is an overstuffed mailbox. When mail and newspapers are littering the yard, it's a safe bet that no one is home. When you travel, make sure that you have your mail and deliveries stopped. The United States Postal Service has an easy way to hold mail that can be accessed online. I have used this service many times. Recurring deliveries like a newspaper or UPS shipments should be held as well.

No Social Media Posts

In explaining the discipline portion of the layered home defense, we discussed how social media could give away valuable information about your whereabouts. So, make sure you don't post anything while you are away. But also, don't post anything about leaving, too.

I've seen plenty of friends who are going on cruises who have a countdown going on their social media page. Not good. I understand wanting to share the joy and excitement of an upcoming trip, but you have share it in person – not where everyone can see it. You can't guarantee who will see your post and what they'll do with this important information. Play it safe.

Hiding Valuables

When a home is burglarized, the first place thieves go is to the master bedroom. Why? Think about what you have in your master bedroom. Typically, this is where jewelry, cash, and firearms are stored. Thieves don't want to spend a lot of time in a home. The chances of being caught increase the longer an invasion lasts. The FBI estimates that the average break-in lasts 8-12 minutes. This means they'll target the value areas first.

Also, near the master bedroom is usually a bathroom. Thieves will most likely ransack your bathroom looking for medication. Don't try and hide valuable items in the bathroom. The old Rolex in a zippy bag in the toilet tank trick has been around for a while, so the bad guys know to look there. Creativity is key to keeping your valuables safe.

A great way to keep your valuables safe is by hiding them in unconventional places. Before leaving for a trip, take a few moments to hide a few valuables, just in case. Book safes are popular. These metal safes are made to look like books but are really hollow metal boxes a with keyed entry. When the book safe sits on a shelf with other books, it blends in and won't raise an alarm. However, if discovered, they can be carried off and opened later.

Another suggestion is to hide items in a new package of paper towels. Individually wrapped paper towels can be opened from the bottom freeing up the hollow cardboard tube for easy access. Small items like jewelry or cash can be stuffed up the tube. Simply tape the bottom of the plastic back up and set the roll in the pantry. No one is the wiser.

When looking to store valuable items in your home, a safe comes to mind. Safes can store anything, from valuable documents to firearms. There is a safe for every need. I recommend that every family store their valuable documents in a fireproof safe, hidden in the house. Small, fireproof safes can be carried out by thieves for opening at another location. But if the safe is not in the master bedroom, say in the bottom of a linen closet, then the chances of them finding it are diminished.

Floor and wall safes should hold up to most prying attacks, and since they are inside a part of your home, it is much harder to remove for opening later. To make sure important papers and jewelry are secure all the time, a safe deposit box at your local bank may be the best option. If you own a firearm, it must be locked up when not in use. Be sure to have a safe rated for the contents you have.

Take a Picture of Your Back Door

This one may sound odd but trust me. (I hope you can by now.) Have you ever left your home and wondered if you locked the back door? Being hundreds of miles away when you have this stomach-sinking thought isn't a good feeling. Before you leave, make sure you take a few photos using your phone to assure yourself that everything has been done.

I know I've been sitting at my desk at work and wondered if I closed my garage door. Then I start to sweat a bit because I know what leaving the garage door open can mean. If you have a security camera that you can access on your phone, you might be able to see large details like an open garage door. But small things like door locks may be hard to see, especially if your cameras can't pan or zoom. That's why taking a few shots of the small details is a good idea.

In addition to photographing your door locks, consider a few other areas as well. Take snapshots of your stove, thermostat, and any other items you secure so you'll have a visual record of what you've done. This should go a long way to helping you relax while you're away and help you remember what you need to reset once you return home.

Going on vacation is meant to be a relaxing time for everyone. If you do your due diligence and take the time to secure your home properly, then you'll feel much more comfortable while you're out of town with your family. Kick back and relax, you deserve it.

HOME SECURITY CHECKLIST

Thank you for reading my book. I work hard every day to help families live safer, happier lives. Don't forget to make the most of your reading experience. I've created a printable home security checklist to help you apply the techniques in this book and make small, intentional steps in making your home and family safer. Simply go www.thesecuredad.com/checklist-for-readers today.

BIBLIOGRAPHY

De Becker, Gavin, Protecting the Gift: Keeping Children and Teenagers Safe (and Parents Sane). New York, NY: Dell; Reprint Edition, 2000

Disario, Robert J., Protect Yourself: A Practical Guide to Avoid Becoming a Victim. Independent, 2017

ABOUT THE AUTHOR

Andy Murphy is a family protection writer who has been featured in the CP Journal: Weekly Profile and parenting blogs from the United States to Australia. He is the founder of The Secure Dad LLC, a platform that helps families live safer, more secure lives while enjoying the blessings of life.

Andy is a proud husband and father. Since 2016, he has written more than 100 articles for TheSecureDad.com. He always enjoys interacting with readers on social media.

The Secure Dad on Instagram:
https://www.instagram.com/thesecuredad
The Secure Dad on Twitter:
https://twitter.com/thesecuredad
The Secure Dad on Facebook:
https://www.facebook.com/thesecuredad
#securedad

RECOMMENDED READING

De Becker, Gavin. The Gift of Fear and Other Survival Signals that Protect Us from Violence. New York: Dell, 1999

De Becker, Gavin. Protecting the Gift: Keeping Children and Teenagers Safe (and Parents Sane) Reprint Edition. New York: Dell, 2000.

Disario, Robert J. Protect Yourself: A Practical Guide to Avoid Becoming a Victim. Independently Published, 2017

Van Horne, Patrick and Jason A. Riley. Left of Bang: How the Marine Corps' Combat Hunter Program Can Save Your Life. New York, Black Irish Entertainment LLC., 2014